D0604193

1181 (or 1182)

Francis is born
in Assisi.

1193 (or 1194)

Clare is born
in Assisi.

1202

In a war between Assisi
and Perugia, Assisi is
defeated in the battle
of Collestrado.

1202-1203

Francis is taken
prisoner and
spends one year
in jail in Perugia.

1204

Francis suffers from
a long illness.

1204 (or 1205)

Francis leaves for the
Apulia province with
Gualtiero di Brienne's
army. In Spoleto Francis
has a vision and returns
to Assisi.

1205

The crucifix in San
Damiano speaks to
Francis and tells him
to repair the church.

1206

Called by his father in
the presence of the
bishop, Francis renounces
his inheritance and gives
his fine clothing back
to his father.

1206-1208

Francis works as a scullery
boy in a monastery. He cares
for people with leprosy and
repairs the churches of San
Damiano, San Pietro, and
Portiuncula.

1208, February 24

Francis sews a rough
robe for himself, uses a
rope as a belt, and
begins preaching
barefoot in the streets.

1208

Francis lives at the
Portiuncula, and other
young men join him
there. Francis sends them
out two by two to preach
around the world.

1209 (or 1210)

Francis writes a Rule to
explain his new way of
life. He goes to the pope
to have it approved.

1211 (or 1212)

On Palm Sunday Clare joins Francis and begins the order of the Poor Clares.

1213-1214

In Spain on his way to Morocco, Francis falls ill and returns to the Portiuncula. Clare is nominated abbess of San Damiano monastery.

1215, November

Francis is present at the Fourth Lateran Council. He probably meets with Saint Dominic.

1217, May 5

The friars in the Portiuncula decide new missions.

1219-1220

Francis sails for the East with the Crusaders. In Egypt he meets the Sultan.

1221

Thousands of friars arrive at the Portiuncula.

1223, December 24-25

In Greccio, Francis creates the first live crèche, or nativity scene.

1224, August 15

Francis receives the stigmata, the signs of Christ's suffering.

1224-1225

Francis spends the winter in the monastery where Clare lives. He composes the "Canticle of Brother Sun."

1225-1226

His health grows worse. Feeling that he will soon die, Francis asks to be carried back to the Portiuncula.

1226, October 3

Francis takes off his robe and asks to be laid down on the bare earth. He blesses the friars and then dies.

1253, August 11

Clare dies in San Damiano monastery.

To all the people I met in Assisi who keep Saint Francis's spirit alive.
—B. L.

To Maria Grazia and to all the birds that kept me company.
—G. V.

We all feel that we belong to this story—wherever we were born, wherever we are living, in sweet union with God.

—*Monsignor Pierangelo Sequeri*

© Edizioni Arka, Milan, Italy 2003

This edition published 2004 in the United States of America by
Eerdmans Books for Young Readers
An imprint of Wm. B. Eerdmans Publishing Company
255 Jefferson SE, Grand Rapids, Michigan 49503
P.O. Box 163, Cambridge CB3 9PU U.K.
www.eerdmans.com

05 06 07 08   6 5 4 3 2

Printed in Italy

Library of Congress Cataloging-in-Publication Data

Visconti, Guido. Clare and Francis / written by Guido Visconti, inspired by the biographies and written works of the two saints of Assisi collected in the Franciscan sources; illustrated by Bimba Landmann.
p. cm.

Summary: Reviews the lives and works of two members of the Assisi society, Francis and Clare, who renounced their wealth and founded religious orders dedicated to relying on God and living in peace, poverty, and humility.

ISBN 0-8028-5269-6 (alk. paper)

1. Francis, of Assisi, Saint, 1182-1226—Juvenile literature. 2. Clare, of Assisi, Saint, 1194-1253—Juvenile literature. 3. Christian saints—Italy—Assisi—Biography—Juvenile literature. 4. Assisi, Italy—Biography—Juvenile literature. [1. Francis, of Assisi, Saint, 1182-1226. 2. Clare, of Assisi, Saint, 1194-1253.] I. Landmann, Bimba, ill. II. Title.

BX4700.F6 v57 2004
2003013441

Clare and Francis

Illustrated by Bimba Landmann

Text by Guido Visconti, inspired by the biographies and written works
of the two saints of Assisi collected in the *Franciscan Sources*

Eerdmans Books for Young Readers
Grand Rapids, Michigan • Cambridge, U.K.

Around the year 1200, a few rich people and many poor people lived in Assisi, Italy. Clare was a young girl not only of noble birth, but also of noble heart. Every evening she said to Bona, her nurse, "There is some bread left over from our meal. Let us give it to the poor in the streets."

Many poor people without homes roamed the streets at night. Some rich young people also strolled around the streets in the evening, laughing and singing. One of them, named Francis, was well known in Assisi, partly because he was always very kind to everyone, but also because he spent a lot of money on amusements. The whole town believed that one day Francis would become a rich fabric merchant like his father.

But Francis dreamed of becoming a knight, like the Knights of the Round Table. He had read of their feats, and he too wanted to fight for high ideals. He decided to enter the service of Pope Innocent III and defend the Papal States. First, however, he had to ask his father's permission. His father, Master Bernadone, was jubilant at his son's decision. He was certain his son would show his worth in battle and return covered with glory. That day Master Bernadone also had another reason to be happy. He had just bought some very precious fabrics to sell in his shop. "This one embroidered in gold is for you," he said proudly to his son. "Jacopone, the tailor, will make a magnificent knight's garment for you." Francis began to daydream: he would grip a golden sword and then . . .

"For the love of God, a little charity, sir," begged a man on the threshold of the shop. "Away with you!" said Francis, still lost in his daydream. But he immediately came to his senses. That was no way for a knight to behave. "If this poor man had come asking me a favor in the name of a prince, I would certainly have welcomed him. Instead he comes in the name of God, who is the King of kings. I cannot deny him what he begs," said Francis to himself, grabbing a few coins and running swiftly after the beggar.

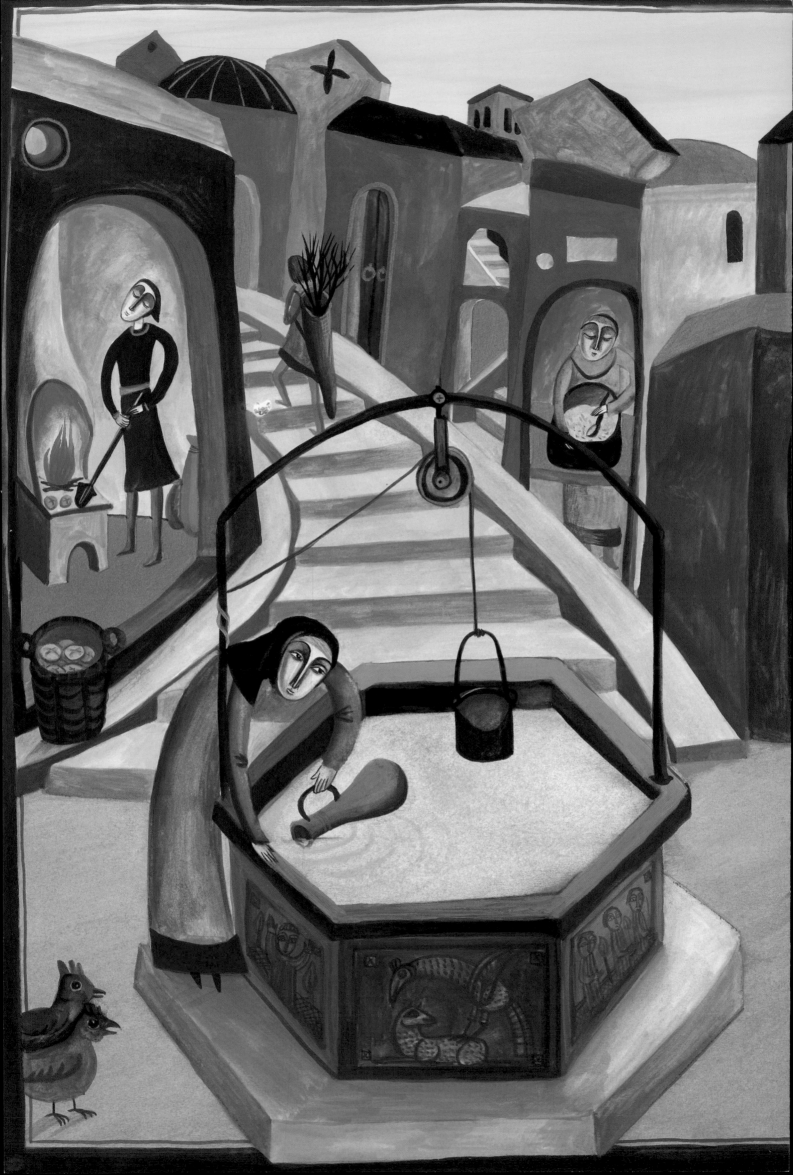

Many more beggars were in the square, too many for the few coins Francis had with him. What could he do? He was grateful to see that Clare had given them food. At times he also gave them food, but he was convinced that a future knight must be even more generous than that. A future knight must be ready to give his own garments to clothe those who have none.

And so, when all the people in Assisi gathered in the streets, they noticed that he was not wearing his costly new garment. He had just given it away to a poor soldier.

"He's mad!" someone whispered.

"He's generous and will do great things for others," Clare murmured to herself.

Everyone agreed that a great future awaited Francis. He thought so too. To those surprised to see him so eager to go to battle, Francis answered, "Don't you know that I am destined to become a great prince?"

But God, who talked to him in a dream that night, had very different plans for him. "Who is it better to follow, a lord or his servant?" God asked Francis.

"Naturally, a lord," Francis replied.

"Then why are you following the servant?"

"My Lord, what do you want me to do?"

"Go back to Assisi, and I will tell you."

Francis woke up with a start and decided not to go and serve the Pope, nor follow his dream of fame and glory. He mounted his horse and galloped back to Assisi.

But once he was in Assisi Francis found it hard to hear the voice of God. Perhaps too many things distracted his thoughts? So Francis gave up everything he had enjoyed—money, fine clothes, delicious food, lively parties with his friends. Very soon many people began wondering why Francis had changed so much. Some made fun of him. "He's gone mad," they said. No one understood. No one except Clare. And Guido, the Bishop of Assisi.

His father certainly didn't understand him. Master Bernardone was furious. How could his son go around filthy and in rags? How dare Francis give his money away to the poor? Master Bernardone rushed to the bishop and said he wanted Francis to give him back his money.

"With pleasure I give you back your money and these garments," replied Francis, taking off his clothes. "From now on I only want to serve God. I will call God, and no one else, Father."

Then the town of Assisi had one more poor person to feed, a young man who had chosen to be poor, a young man who spoke powerful words that could shake the listener to the core. The bishop lovingly covered Francis with his own cloak. Francis asked for a cloth sack to use to make a tunic the color of a common lark, which flies and sings high up in the sky. Master Bernardone, thoroughly offended, took the money and clothes from Francis and walked off. All the people of Assisi were moved by this scene, and some began to understand.

Bernardo, a very rich man, was the first to understand. Soon two others, Peter and Egido, also understood. These men listened to Francis talk about poverty, and they too began to distance themselves from money. They listened as he begged for stones with which to rebuild a church that was in ruins. "Come and help me restore the church of San Damiano," Francis said. "God spoke to me there, saying, 'Go, Francis, and repair my house.'"

These men decided, like Francis, to wear coarse tunics tied at the waist with a cord. And, like him, they traveled barefoot through cities and countryside. To all they met they spoke about God and about how to find peace within oneself. They helped farmers in exchange for bread or went from door to door, bowls in hand, and begged for food. Many made fun of them, but more and more men decided to join Francis.

Clare wanted to follow him too. She, like many others in Assisi, had long admired him, but ever since she had heard him preach, her life was filled with extraordinary light. Francis was not only a humble, generous man who looked after lepers. Francis was, like herself, in love with God. "I too want to live in poverty and at the service of others. But how can I achieve this?" she asked herself. "My mother won't hinder me, but my father will be furious!"

Clare's mind, however, was made up. She would go and visit Francis. She wanted to talk to him and ask his advice. She simply wanted to be near him. She asked Bona, her nurse, to take her to him without her father knowing.

Francis then lived at the Portiuncula, a small abandoned church near Assisi. He lived there with other friars, called brothers. Francis knew that Clare was a generous girl, and he was very pleased to meet her. That day they spent hours talking together, and he invited her to return.

Every time she visited the friars, Clare was surprised to see how well they looked after the flowers, the orchard, and the trees. Francis allowed the friars to cut off only a few branches of these trees for Brother Fire. They also took great care of animals, which Francis also called brothers and sisters.

But what surprised Clare most was the way Francis listened to her, talked to her, and advised her on which path to take.

On Palm Sunday Clare prayed during mass. She prayed so fervently that she didn't notice when the rest of the faithful stood up and walked to the bishop to get their palms. She remained in her seat.

The bishop, who understood Clare's passion, slowly descended the altar, walked toward her, and handed her a palm. Everyone was silent, stunned by this gesture which the bishop wouldn't even have bestowed upon a king. "Who is Clare to deserve such an honor?" they asked themselves.

If the people of Assisi had seen her that same evening walking alone from her father's house, they would have asked themselves, "What is she doing? Where is she going? Is she mad?"

Clare wasn't mad. Clare was free. She was sure of her path and wanted to follow it. Her father would at long last stop looking for a husband for her. From now on she would devote herself only to God. She went to Francis, who was expecting her.

She discarded her beautiful wool dress and put on a coarse tunic made by the friars. She let Francis cut her long hair, as the flames of torches reached high up toward the sky.

Clare, however, could not remain forever with Francis and the other friars. Francis took her to the church of San Damiano.

He was extremely fond of that church. He had built it himself, begging for stone after stone. And he had even foreseen it would become a convent. This, then, was Clare's new home, the place where she had decided to live forever, withdrawn from the world.

Instead of withdrawing, Francis knew it was time for him to journey into the world. His reputation was spreading quickly, so he went out talking to everyone he met about peace, poverty, and humility. He told people that they should feel love for all of creation—not only for the lilies in the fields, but also for stones or a worm crossing the road. He talked about this love with great joy because, owning nothing, he felt happy and free. Even the birds listened to Francis. "Brother Birds," he said, "you must praise your Creator. You don't sow, harvest, or weave, and yet he has given you feathers to cover you, wings to fly, and everything else you need."

Not everyone found it easy to put Francis's words into practice. Nevertheless, more and more young men became his followers. Francis sent them off to preach to people in the four corners of the earth. "Go, but don't take anything with you—no knapsack, no bread, no money," he told them using words taken from the Gospel. "As pilgrims, go happily and merrily."

Then he too crossed the sea.

Francis went to the East, though not to fight alongside the Crusaders. He wanted only to bring a message of love and peace.

In Egypt, the Sultan received him with great honor.

Francis returned to Italy. There he visited many towns and villages and preached to both people and animals.

Before Francis arrived in Gubbio, only a few people believed that he had the gift of talking to and of being understood by animals. But after his visit there, everyone believed it.

For months the people of Gubbio had been living in terror of a huge, ferocious wolf. The wolf attacked both people and animals.

Francis went to pay the wolf a visit. "Come here, Brother Wolf," he said to him. "You have done a great deal of harm in the neighborhood. Everyone here is terrified of you. You must make peace with the people of Gubbio. You must no longer harm them, and they will no longer persecute you." The wolf walked up to Francis, lowered its head, and, tame as a lamb, gave Francis his paw.

Then everyone, even little children, dared to walk into the square where Francis and the wolf waited for them. "Listen," Francis told them, "Brother Wolf here has promised to make peace with you. Now you must promise that every day you will give him all the food he needs." This was a just peace, and the people, full of wonder, were happy. Many were surprised at the power of love between Francis and all creatures.

Back in San Damiano, Clare too knew the power of love. Many women, rich and poor, asked to be allowed to enter the convent. Clare welcomed them all, including her two sisters, Agnes and Beatrice, and her mother. Other women brought her their sick children, and Clare often was able to cure them.

One day Francis arrived. He was very ill, and his eyes hurt so much that he had to live in a dark room. He could no longer see the sunlight or the stars shining at night, but he still thanked God for all the beauty of creation. One day he said, "I want to compose a canticle, a song for all of God's creatures."

Turning to his friars he said, "We are all blind. It is the Lord who gives us light during the day in the shape of the sun, and in the shape of fire at night. We must always thank our Creator for these and all God's creatures." Then he said, "Praise to you, oh Lord, with all your creatures, especially Brother Sun."

And Francis did not stop. He sang not one praise, but many—for Sister Moon, for Brother Wind, for Sister Water, for Brother Fire, and one for Mother Earth. He even sang one for those who are incapable of living peacefully on this earth. When Francis discovered that the two most powerful men in Assisi, the bishop and the mayor, lived as enemies rather than as brothers, he added to his canticle, "Praise to you, Lord, for those who pardon for love of you."

The song Francis wrote was full of joy. He named it the "Canticle of Brother Sun" and composed a melody for it. Since he could no longer go out and preach, Francis sent his friars, saying, "Go! Go and sing the 'Canticle of Brother Sun.'"

Friars still sing it today, almost 800 years later, for this message of peace and love lives on.

And the feast of Christmas, too, lives on. Even today people often celebrate Christmas the way Francis first celebrated it at Greggio in 1223. There he recreated the manger scene, with the cave, the donkey, the bull, and the straw where Mary and Joseph laid the baby Jesus, the Son of God, born on earth poor and humble.

Canticle of Brother Sun

Translation from the original Italian

Most high, all-powerful, all good Lord! All praise is yours, all glory,
all honor, and all blessing. To you alone, Most High, do they belong.
All praise be yours, my Lord, through all that you have made.

And first my Lord, Brother Sun, who brings the day; and light you give to us through him.
How beautiful he is, how radiant in all his splendor! Of you, Most High, he bears the likeness.

All praise be yours, my Lord, through Sister Moon and Stars;
in the heavens you have made them, bright and precious and fair.

All praise be yours, my Lord, through Brothers Wind and Air, and fair and stormy,
all the weather's moods, by which you cherish all that you have made.

All praise be yours, my Lord, through Sister Water so useful, lowly, precious, and pure.

All praise be yours, my Lord, through Brother Fire, through whom you brighten up the night.
How beautiful he is, how joyful! Full of power and strength.

All praise be yours, my Lord, through Sister Earth, our mother, who feeds us in her sovereignty
and produces various fruits and colored flowers and herbs.

All praise be yours, my Lord, through those who grant pardon for love of you;
through those who endure sickness and trial.

Happy those who endure in peace; by you, Most High, they will be crowned.

All praise be yours, my Lord, from Sister Death, from whose embrace no mortal can escape.
Woe to those who die in mortal sin! Happy those she finds doing your will!
The second death can do no harm to them.

Praise and bless my Lord, and give him thanks,
and serve him with great humility.

Canticle of Brother Sun

Translation from United States Catholic Conference

O most High, almighty, good Lord God,
to you belong praise, glory, honor, and all blessing!

Praised be my Lord God with all creatures; and especially our brother the sun,
which brings us the day and the light; fair is he, and shining with a great splendor;

O Lord, he signifies you to us! Praised be our Lord for our sister the moon,
and for the stars, which God has set clear and lovely in heaven.

Praised be my Lord for our brother the wind, and for air and cloud,
calms and all weather, by which you uphold in life all creatures.

Praised be my Lord for our sister water,
which is very serviceable to us, and humble, and precious, and clean.

Praised be our Lord for brother fire, by which you give us light in the darkness;
and he is bright, and pleasant, and mighty, and strong.

Praised be my Lord for our mother, the earth, which sustains us and keeps us
and yields diverse fruits, and flowers of many colors, and grass.

Praised be my Lord for all those who pardon one another for God's love's sake,
and who endure weakness and tribulation; blessed are they who peaceably shall endure,
for you, O most High, shall give them a crown!

Praised be our Lord for our sister, the death of the body,
from which no one escapes.

Woe to him who dies in mortal sin! Blessed are they who are found walking
by your most holy will, for the second death shall have no power to do them harm.

Praise you and bless you the Lord and give thanks
to God and serve God with great humility.